How to Survive
a Horseriding Tour
in Iceland

How to Survive a Horseriding Tour in Iceland
© Eva Mueller 2014

Publisher: Steinegg ehf.
Reykjavík 2014

Pictures and text © Eva Mueller 2014
Printing and binding: Oddi, Iceland

© Steinegg ehf. 2014

ISBN 978-9935-421-43-2

Eva Mueller

How to Survive
a Horseriding Tour
in Iceland

STEINEGG
www.steinegg.is

The Main Characters

charm

tiny ears

beard

wind in the mane

pride

endless stamina

lots of extra gaits

mountain goat

The Icelandic Horse

tousled hair

farmer's tan

„Gore-Tex is for women and tourists"

„water" bottle

leather gear

bow legs

proper boots

The Icelandic Cowboy

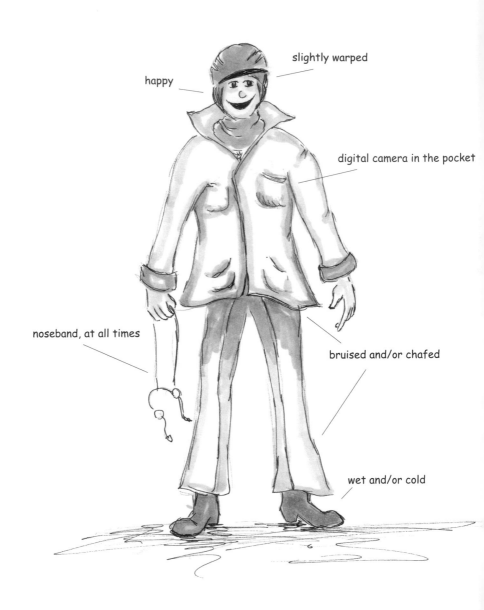

slightly warped

happy

digital camera in the pocket

noseband, at all times

bruised and/or chafed

wet and/or cold

The Icelandic Horse riding Tourist

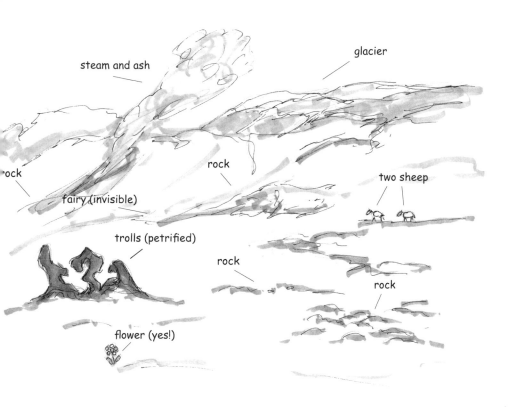

steam and ash

glacier

ock

rock

fairy (invisible)

two sheep

trolls (petrified)

rock

rock

flower (yes!)

Iceland...

Don't be intimidated by the staff...

...They are all really nice!

Some general advice

Please refrain from plaiting the horse's tail...

...or mane!

Never call them "ponies".

Well...
There's going to be a little rain...
A little wind... A little sun...
Maybe a little hail... Maybe very hot...

Never ask about the weather.

With an Icelandic Horse...

...you'll always know which direction the wind is coming from.

Due to the scarcity of trees and fences in Iceland,
your horse may try and make use of you as a scratching post.
However, you shouldn't let him do this...

...The reins might come off.

He is hardly ever successful with this...

...so you can just imagine how much he enjoys rolling around!

You won't succeed in baiting your horse with an apple...

...But what he really enjoys is a good scratch under the mane!

Ready to Go

Wear your rain gear with pride!

... Even though the raintrousers tend to ride up in a bundle,
thus proving rather ineffective ...

Icelandic Horses are used to being handled from both sides.
Just try mounting from the left once in while...

...It is good practice for your balance!

For easier mounting, you can try to lead your horse next to a rock and get up from there...

...Or perhaps not.

There is something called the classical dressage position.
Many people aspire to this, more or less sucessfully...

...And then there is the classical Icelandic slouch.

It is not advisable to ride with short stirrups,
even if you're used to doing so at home...

...And just forget about rising trot.

There is a lot of standing about and waiting, so you may sometimes
feel like a henchman of the Wild West in between chases...

...but that doesn't make you even remotely look like
Clint Eastwood.

Even if it is surprisingly warm and sunny at the start of the ride...

...it is essential to wear gloves and thermal underwear
when riding in the highlands!

Sometimes the riding tracks are very well trodden...

...Sometimes it is hard to say if there is a path at all...

But then, the Icelandic Horse is justly famous for its astounding ability
to climb upwards...

...or downwards.

The Many Gaits of the Icelandic Horse

The Tölt - It will make you happy.

The Trot - Unpopular but necessary.

The Flying Pace - You'll feel very smug if you master this.

The Piggy Pace - No reason to feel smug whatsoever.

The Canter - Mostly occurs when your horse is tired of tölting and wants to rest for a while...

The Gallop - Should be avoided because the Icelandic horses
take it as a cue to run races...

The Walk is rare on an Icelandic Horseriding Tour,
so it should be made use of when it occurs...

But don't forget to look at the landscape once in a while in
between taking pictures.

Out there

There are certain similarities between someone
who rides an Icelandic Horse...

...and someone who rides a heavy motorbike...

Due to the scarcity of trees and even shrubs in Iceland,
the walk to the toilet can be a long, lonely one...

...or not so lonely after all.

It is however essential to always relieve yourself before a long ride...

...You will soon realize why...

It is hard to get your horse to stay put while you're trying
to take his picture while holding his reins...

...so most of these kinds of portraits look very similar...

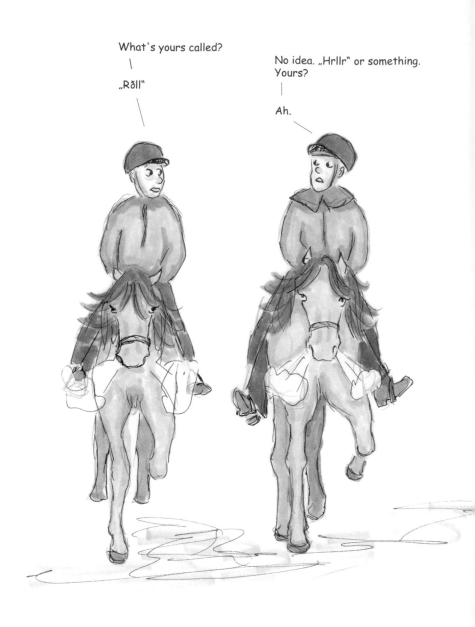

Most of the horses' names are of course unpronounceable...

...with just a few exceptions.

There may be more than one spot that hurts at the end of the day...

...Your fellow riders will be happy to compare notes.

Horses related to each other will often stand
close to each other in the paddock...

...and then gang up on single horses.

Herna er Hvítsmári.. og svo Skógarsmári...
Rauðsmári

Here is Rauðsmári for you...

64

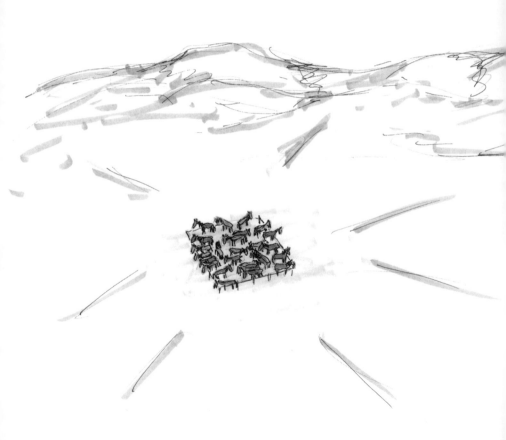

There are paddocks in the middle of the Highlands
where the horses are fenced in during a break.

Your Fellow Riders

The Americans are good at Western Riding - which the
Icelandic Horses have never heard of.

The French are good at miraculously staying spotless throughout.

The English are good at pointing out the astoundingly obvious.

The Finns know how to make use of the Hot Pot!

The Germans just regress into general happy immaturity.

Sometimes you have to go without a shower for a few days,
so everybody dreams of the same thing simultaneously...

On arrival at the hut, the scarcity of working showers
poses a problem, however...

Be that as it may, when it finally happens, this shower feels fantastic...

...and you will all happily meet again in the Hot Pot!

Will we have an opportunity to go shopping?

...and do a bit of painting?

...and gather herbs?

There is no shame in asking questions...

It is appreciated if you try to speak Icelandic. But then, Icelanders are not really used to hearing their language spoken (badly) by foreigners.

Many guests behave like happy children!

And many guests behave like children in other aspects...

Features of Iceland

The Icelanders have a few specialties they like to scare their guests with.

But they also have brennivin.

Being invisible, fairies are hard to spot. They may get slightly miffed if you go traipsing through their living room...

To spot trolls, however, you don't need any imagination at all...

It is best to enjoy and make the most of your horseriding tour, so...
enjoy the soft, sandy riding ground of the Emstrur desert...

...particularly if you're riding at the back of the group.

Enjoy the Icelandic wind...

Enjoy the Icelandic rain...

Enjoy the Icelandic scenery...

...as it rushes past.

But most of all, enjoy the Icelandic horse. It is he who carries you through this wonderful experience and makes it all possible!

Back in Reykjavik: How to spot the difference between a tourist and a local...

*I'd like to thank Vilborg Halldórsdottir,
for giving me confidence in this project.*

Julia Priestley, for helping me with the language.

*And last, but by no means least,
everyone I ever met on a Horseriding Tour in Iceland.*